FROM LAND'S END
❧ ❧ T O ❧ ❧
JOHN-O'-GROATS,

BY

GEORGE H. ALLEN,

THE VEGETARIAN LONG
DISTANCE RECORD WALKER.

❧

BEING AN ACCOUNT OF HIS
RECORD WALK, IN WHICH
HE ACCOMPLISHED 908½
MILES IN 16 DAYS,
21 HOURS, AND
33 MINUTES.

❧

LONDON:
L. N. Fowler & Co., 7, Imperial Arcade,
Ludgate Circus.

PAISLEY:
The Progressive Press, 12, High Street.
1905.

CONTENTS.

❧

Anderson 16 May 1934

PREFACE.

❧

BECAUSE Vegetarianism has done so much for me, I am willing to give my best to the advancement of its principles.

I do not suggest that feats of endurance in themselves constitute the highest form of propaganda, but they have the advantage of being very real argument for the cause.

This book is sent forth at the request of several friends as a record of the greatest athletic feat of my life.

GEO. H. ALLEN,

Whiteway,

Stroud.

May, 1905.

FROM LAND'S END
—— TO ——
JOHN O' GROAT'S.

A FEAT of endurance of such magnitude as the one under notice, must only be undertaken by a man with a wide knowledge of athletics, and in the finest trained condition. Otherwise the result may prove disastrous.

Even with my varied athletic experience, I had, at the outset, greatly under-estimated the task before me.

Wisdom born of defeat schooled me; success at length rewarded my efforts, and recompensed me for all my labour, as the following account will show :—

On May 25th, 1903, I started from The Royal Exchange, Glasgow, with the object of walking 1,000 miles in 20 days. After covering 455 miles in 9 days, I was reluctantly compelled to retire, my feet being in such a swollen and blistered state, that I found it impossible to get my boots on when I arose on the morning of the tenth day.

This was a great disappointment to me, but scarcely as great as when I again failed in a similar attempt in the September following.

This time I did a splendid performance from a strictly athletic point of view, namely:— 420 miles within 7 days, but still the object striven for was not reached.

I now decided to retire finally from active participation in athletic feats, but Necessity, in the form of a record established by Dr. Deighton, forced me to again enter the lists.

In the spring of 1904, this well-known athlete walked from Land's End to John o' Groat's in 24 days 4 hours. His chief sustenance en-route was a much-advertised meat juice. The credit which should have been given to the undoubted courage of Dr. Deighton was largely claimed by the company who ran the whole affair financially.

To prove that flesh foods generally and meat juices in particular are utterly unnecessary for such a feat of endurance, now seemed to be a

task it was my duty to perform, in view of my
two previous undertakings. My record walk
was the result.

✄ ✄

Preparing for the Ordeal.

✄

IN the month of June, 1904, special training was commenced.

My garden work at home claimed my
attention as usual, for Nature will brook no
delay, nor await the convenience of any one.

Honestly, the training walks were anything
but enjoyable, as a rule. Although I knew
that the 150 to 200 miles which I walked
every week was none too much, I felt I was
wasting my time largely when walking. I
knew that this outlook was foolish; but I could
not bring myself into any other frame of mind
The greatest puzzle to me during my period of
training was Geo. H. Allen.

The drudgery of training was such, that I
had to write down each Sunday my daily walking distances for the following week; and these
lists were adhered to rigidly. I was learning
what it meant to conquer the body. Heat or

storm, rain or shine, in suitable or unsuitable weather, I kept myself at it. The consequence was that by the time the starting day came round, I was in superb physical condition, such as I had never previously enjoyed.

On Saturday, August 27th, I arrived in Penzance, in readiness for the start on the following Monday, full of confidence; but in my most enthusiastic moments (and I have many) no idea of beating the record by $7\frac{1}{2}$ days ever entered my head.

A quiet Saturday evening, and a walk of 10 miles along with my cycling attendant on Sunday morning, brought us to Land's End ready for the morrow.

Sunday was passed quietly away, then we both retired to rest shortly after 9 p.m.

As I lay in bed the flashes from the Longships Lighthouse, $1\frac{1}{4}$ miles distant, could be distinctly seen. Once the headlights of a northward bound vessel came into my line of view, as it rounded Land's End.

I lay a thinking for some time, wondering what the next three weeks had in store for me. Eventually I sank into a dreamless sleep, to awake at 3.30 a.m. the following morning.

First Day—Monday August 29th.

*

Land's End to St. Austell.—50 Miles.

*

THE start had been originally fixed for 4 a.m., but a slight hitch in the arrangements hindered us an hour.

Punctually at 5 a.m., in the quiet and calm of the grey morning, after having our book signed, the word to " Go " was given, and the start was made.

Everything had been carefully thought out by me long ere this, and the daily distances and stopping-places for each night settled, at any rate for the earlier stages of the walk. During the first week I kept strictly to my book, but later it was exceeded.

The exact route mapped out by " Dr. Deighton" was followed, which is much farther than the one usually favoured by End-to-End record-breakers ; but to come back to the walk proper.

The morning air had such an exhilarating effect upon me, that it was with difficulty I was able to keep myself from going at five miles per hour, for, be it known that when over 900 miles lies before one, the physical powers have to be conserved, or at any rate not squandered, or failure is inevitable.

My attendant on his bicycle caught me up before I had gone a mile.

The knapsack, which contained a complete change of clothing along with other trifles indespensible to such an undertaking, was carried by him. Also the book for the reception of signatures of people who saw us pass en route.

This is of the greatest importance, in view of the many bogus records the public have had foisted upon them. In duty to the said public we publish our list of signatures.

With a cheery "How do you feel?" my attendant caught me up. He also felt the responsibility of his position, as I could tell by the eager look upon his face.

A little further on, he hurriedly dismounted and flung a horseshoe after me,—a token of good luck.

Now, I have always prided myself on my absolute freedom from all superstition, but this little rusty token picked up by my friend cheered me more than I care to admit. The Irish blood in me showed itself.

The surface of the road was in perfect condition hereabouts, free from mud and dust. A little later, under an avenue of trees which stretched for some considerable distance, it was rather greasy. Now we emerged into the open again with Penzance not far ahead.

The town hall clock at this place (10 miles) was passed at 7.20.

At this early hour the sun had considerable power, foretelling a sultry day. The shops were not as yet open ; but a few business early birds wending their way slowly along the streets enquired politely where I was bound for, and were interested when told.

The first stopping-place was at Hayle, 8 miles further. This town was reached at 9 o'clock —exactly the time I intended arriving.

A breakfast consisting of eggs, white bread, tomatoes, and weak tea was here partaken of, and the journey was resumed after a halt of half-an-hour.

At 10.45, Cambourne (23½ miles) was left behind. The thriving town of Redruth, with its electric trams, and Chacewater were passed ; and by 1.45, the city of Truro was entered. The inhabitants turned out in full force, quite a crowd collecting while we were having our dinner.

One hour-and-a-quarter for this meal; and amidst a good round of encouragement, the 14 miles stretch remaining to be covered that day, was entered upon. The heat was now intense; indeed, it was one of the hottest days of a very hot summer; but it seemed to have little or no effect upon me.

Grampound (44¾ miles) was passed at 4.50, and by 6.15 St. Austell was reached, and the first day's journey ended.

A lecture at 7.30 (which was attended by a large and eager crowd) rounded off this day, and I retired to rest at 9.30.

❧ ❧

Second Day—Tuesday, Aug. 30th.

❧

St. Austell to Plymouth, 39 Miles.
Total—89 Miles.

❧

THIS was the smallest day's walk on the whole tour. I had determined not to overtax myself the first week, aiming at about 45 miles per day. As there was no convenient stopping place for the first day at this distance, I had decided when making out my list, to reach St. Austell and have an easy walk on Tuesday. Besides, Plymouth struck me as a good town for a meeting. Hence the arrangement.

From a record-breaking point of view it was throwing time away to stay here. However, this is overrunning the story.

Before retiring for the night, we decided, in view of the possibility of another hot day, to make an early start for Plymouth next morning, and take a long rest during the heat of the day, if necessary.

The great bane of long distance walking is blistered feet, and hot weather has a very bad effect in this direction.

We planned the start for 5 o'clock, but 15 minutes prior to this I was on my way once more.

Past experience had taught me that it is most difficult to find the way out of a strange town in the early morning when very few people are about.

To avoid any possibility of making a mistake, I had instructed my cyclist to *find* the way out before he went to bed.

St. Blazey was the next town to St. Austel, and when the first man my attendant asked, informed him that it was *"straight out,"* to this place, he concluded that his instructions were all-sufficient. He had yet to learn that the inhabitants of towns are often very much at sea as to where they live.

As a rule, there is no *"straight out"* of towns.

Scarcely had I gone 100 yards " *straight out,"* when the first check met me in the shape of a stone building. The road here forked.

A sorter at the Post Office put me on the way again with another *"straight out ! "* Another half-a-mile, and another division of the road.

I took the right-hand way, which was wrong. My cyclist, following later, took the left : he was right ; but we had lost each other. A mile or two later my mistake was apparent : I had reached the sea-shore.

No one seemed stirring at this early hour, and things were unpleasant to say the least. In my dilemma I looked around, and just as I had resolved to awaken someone, I caught sight of a man in uniform with a telescope fixed in my direction.

Quickly I made for him, and was a minute or two later undergoing the scrutiny of the coastguard.

When he was satisfied that I was not a foreign spy or anything dangerous, I was directed, very politely, on my journey. No "*straight out*" this time, but : " Take the road to the right, round by the chapel, and the next turning to the right."

A miserable drizzling rain commenced about this time, which added to my discomfort. My cyclist early became aware that he had missed me, and, whenever possible, left news of his whereabouts.

At Lostwithiel (8½ miles) the inhabitants are evidently early risers, for they were astir when I passed through. Reliable news of my attendant was obtained here. The rain had now ceased, and by the time I had overtaken my cyclist, pushing his machine up a hill about 1½ miles long, my clothing was dry once more.

All was now right, except that I had covered two or three miles that did not count.

My appetite was keen indeed, and so my friend was instructed to go forward and order breakfast.

By 9 o'clock we had both settled down to a substantial meal, provided by a kindly baker's wife at East Taphouse.

There was no particular hurry to-day, and so we had a rest of 1¼ hours, and then made for Liskeard (19¾ miles for the day).

At Polbathic, 9 miles from Plymouth, dinner was served. Here for the first time I tasted " Devonshire Junket," since when I have been loud in my praises of this delicious food.

At Tor Point we were delayed twenty minutes waiting for the ferry. The day's walking was finally ended at 5.45 p.m.

✿ ✿

Third Day—Wednesday, Aug. 31st.

✿

Plymouth to Exeter,—47½ Miles.
Total—136½ Miles.

✿

ACCOMPANIED by a friend who had volunteered to pioneer us out of the town, we made a start for this day at 4.50 a.m.

At Ridgeway he left us. He had put us right on the main road. We should have been certain to have gone wrong had he not been with us, finger-posts being conspicuous by their absence. A driving rain, which lasted about an hour, was very welcome after the heat of the two previous days. It settled the dust splendidly, and thereby tempered the heat which followed.

Brentbridge (15¾ miles) had been fixed upon as the stopping place for our first meal. When my attendant left to order breakfast, it was with the understanding that he came back again to meet me ; but he did not work exactly to orders. Instead of riding back, he left his machine outside the hotel door, thinking it was impossible for me to miss the very conspicuous green handles ; but this is what happened. As I passed through the village, I looked for a cyclist riding to meet me, and missed his machine, which must have been hidden behind a cart, or something of the kind ; at any rate, I lost my breakfast, and was forced to go to Totnes (23½ miles) for a meal. *Moral :*—" It is the little foxes that spoil the vines." When we did get a meal at a neat refreshment house, I was amply repaid for my wait, as both the host and hostess were anxious to do all they could to help us, placing their best room at our disposal.

At the Clifford Hotel, Chudleigh, famous for having been patronised by royalty on more than one occasion, a fine dinner was provided. The hostess of this place introduced us to the editress of the local paper, who pinned a favour in my coat and wished me " good luck" en route.

Six miles before entering Exeter, a fine view of the town was obtained. There a finger-post which read " Three miles to White-way " reminded me of my quiet retreat in the Cotswolds, and of those awaiting my return there.

The Osborne Hotel, Exeter, was entered at 6.18 p.m. In the bathroom I was rather startled to find that my right heel showed distinct signs of blistering. This alarmed me somewhat ; but my anxiety was needless, as the next two days proved.

Fourth Day.—Thursday, September 1st.

Exeter to Bridgwater—43½ Miles. Total—180 Miles.

I FELT in excellent trim on arising this morning, with the exception of a slight soreness of the right heel.

By a quarter to five we had made a start, and again we went the wrong way, but did not go far out of our course. A farmer in a waggon just happened upon us at a critical point. We should have gone through Broad Clyst, but this village was left a little to our right. This was the only point where we missed going by the exact rout mapped out.

Two miles before reaching Cullompton, our first stopping place for the day, a rude reminder of old times was met. Several women and girls wending their way to work passed us. I knew at once by their manner and bearing that they were victims of the cursed factory system. We learned while at breakfast that it was as I thought.

Cullompton is one of the best of many peaceful places in lovely Devonshire. Instead of the gutters being choked with refuse, as we often see in that latest product of civilisation, *the up-to-date town*, a stream of clear water runs on either side of the street, giving a delightful sense of coolness on a hot day.

I fell to wondering why people leave this life of peace and quiet, so conducive to the development of all that is best in us, to go to towns and cities to lose both body and soul in the fierce race for wealth; and whether those who have done this, and have been successful in the efforts, in a material sense, do not in their moments of reason repine for the peace and purity of the life and home they have left behind.

Taunton (38 miles) was reached and dinner partaken of.   Again we had plenty of time. Indeed, I felt that we were wasting it ; but in my calculations I had not reckoned on being in such splendid physical condition.   Just over an hour-and-a-half was spent here, Bridgwater being reached at 5.45 p.m.

An enthusiastic cyclist accompanied us all the way from Taunton to Bridgwater, and among other interesting pieces of local information he told us that all the bathbrick used the world over comes from the latter place, being made out of a sand peculiar to this place. I retired rather early, but the church bells, just outside my bedroom window, kept me awake. Eventually they ceased ; I fell asleep, and awoke at 3.55 a.m. on the morning of the fifth day.

Fifth Day.—Friday, Sept. 2nd.

Bridgwater to Stone.—49 Miles. Total—229 Miles.

NO time was cut to waste. Fifteen minutes after arising we were on our way. At Highbridge, which was reached by 6.10 a.m., we were one day in advance of Dr. Deighton's time at the same point. This gave me something substantial to work upon, and was very encouraging.

My blistered foot was painful, and this was the worst day of the first week.

The breakfast at Cross (18 miles) was not enjoyed very much : and the dinner at Bristol still less. I was wondering all the day whether my feet would mend.

The heat was intense during the greater part of the day, and the rest of two hours at Bristol, while we had dinner and my attendant had his machine overhauled, was very welcome.

When walking was resumed at 3.15, I felt anything but cheerful.

The machine had not been repaired, but put out of order altogether, and my attendant had to push it all the way, with the exception of short distances down hills, all the way from Bristol to Stone, 16 miles or more.

The cool of the evening now came on. My feet had righted themselves, and by the time Stone was reached I was in fine form, finishing the day very cheerful.

While we were having tea at the only inn the place boasts of, a neighbouring farmer entertained us by telling, amongst other items, how cider was made. His jovial face and contented look did us good. We had our chance later, when we told him that neither of us ever ate meat. This was a huge surprise for our friend, and before he left us he pressed us to take a basket of choice Victoria plums.

These came in handy on the following day, when we were obliged to miss our dinner.

A native repairer made a sound job of the bicycle; and we retired to rest easy in our minds once more.

❧ ❧

Sixth Day.—Saturday, Sept. 3rd.

❧

Stone to Worcester,—44 Miles.
Total—273 Miles.

❧

BY 4.35 we had made a start in the cold rain foɪ Gloucester, 18 miles distant, where we intended staying for our breakfast.

The thought that my mother, wife and family would meet me there made the distance appear short.

At 8.35 we were seated in a comfortable refreshment room, awaiting the arrival of the party. It seemed an age since I had seen them, and I mentally resolved that when this walk was out of hand, so to speak, I would never undertake anything of the same magnitude again. At heart I am a home bird, and never quite at ease after I have been absent twenty-four hours.

Presently those for whom I had been anxiously awaiting arrived, and a happy hour-and-a-half was spent; but duty is duty, and at 10 o'clock I set out for Worcester, 26 miles distant.

At Tewkesbury several people enquired how I felt; they had seen me before on my last attempt and were anxious about me. We had intended taking dinner at Sevenstoke, but the one who had said that he would order the meal had not fulfilled his promise, so we had to pass on.

The farmer's plums now came in handy. I kept going without a rest until Worcester was reached, and by 4.10 p.m. the first week's walk had come to an end.

My cycling friend left me here, to attend to his business at home.

I was in a bit of a fix. I had, however, anticipated this muddle for some time and was partly prepared. A telegram to a friend in Birmingham secured me an attendant at once, the best one I have ever had on any feat of endurance undertaken by me.

It will be noticed that the daily average this week works out at 45½ miles.

Sunday, September 4th,

W AS observed as a day of rest. All record-breakers, I believe, rest on Sunday. It was a most anxious day for me. Here I was awaiting an attendant whom I had only met on one occasion ; all previous arrangements wanting overhauling.

However, after months of training and calculating, I did not intend to be daunted by a small thing. Nothing short of an earthquake would have stopped me now ; on the contrary, I determined to reach Glasgow the following Saturday, if possible. There I knew friends would be awaiting me to give me all the help I needed.

Attendant No. 2 arrived on Sunday afternoon, and my plans were placed before him. He entered heartily into the spirit of the walk, especially when he knew that 80 miles had been cut off the record already.

Seventh Day.—Monday, September 5th.

*

Worcester to Stafford.—53½ Miles.
Total—326½ Miles.

*

NOW that the disappointments of the first week were left behind, it was with a light heart that I started on this day from the Central Restaurant, Worcester, where Sunday had been spent.

According to my book, Penkridge was to be the stopping place for the night, but I decided, if possible, to reach Stafford, 6½ miles beyond.

If Glasgow, 320 miles distant from Worcester, was to be reached by Saturday, no less distance than this would suffice. My courage was screwed to the sticking-point when at 4.20 a.m. I set off for the second week.

The morning was lovely; my cyclist was cheerful; and we decided to put a good distance behind our backs before our first meal time. The surface of the road between Worcester and Birmingham was good.

By the time Droitwich (7 miles) was reached I felt in perfect condition. One or two visitors, evidently there for the benefit to be derived from the famous brine baths, were about and looked after me as if they envied me my vitality. Health is its own advertisement.

Five miles further on, several workmen were enjoying an early cup of coffee in the well-kept coffee-house at Bromsgrove. A policeman in plain clothes rather reluctantly signed our book here. The importance of his position had evidently grown upon him, for he explained that "he was very careful what he put his name to." My friend, the cyclist, assured him that all was straight and above-board, then he signed his name with a flourish.

Northfield Institute, 20 miles since starting that morning, was reached by 9 o'clock. We had our breakfast at the fine coffee-house, built by Mr. Cadbury, of cocoa fame. Mr. and Mrs. Ketley, the good people in charge, had become interested in the walk, from reading accounts in the *Daily News*. When we paid our bill they would only accept the bare cost of the food, and pressed us to take some fruit to eat on the way. Thoughts of George Fox, and his leather suit were prompted by the quiet maid in a plain, neat gown, who waited upon us, and also by the kindly advice of one of the

" Friends " at parting, to be honest at all costs.
The world owes more to the Quakers than it
will ever realise.

When the famous Leicestershire shoemaker
set out on that eventful morning, 200 years
ago, in search of the Holy Grail, the powers of
evil received a blow from which they will never
recover.

The clocks of Birmingham were striking
eleven as we went along Corporation Street,
Birmingham (26 miles).

By 1 o'clock Walsall (36¾ miles) was reached.
The heat of the sun was by this time intense,
and my feet burned as they came in contact
with the dusty road.   People were hurrying
home to their dinners as if they had only a
few hours to live and do their life's work in.

At Bloxwich, 1½ miles further, we tried in
vain to get a meal.   The pavements were vile,
and I was glad to leave this town behind.

When we were having dinner at Cannock
(42¾ miles) we were interviewed by a local
reporter, and felt glad when he took his departure and left us in peace.   So well had I
been going all the day that it was only 2.40 p.m.
when Cannock was reached.

At 4 o'clock the last 10¾ miles for the day was entered upon. Penkridge was entered at 5 o'clock, and for the first time I was ahead of my book-plans. A pleasant-looking man in charge of a smart horse and trap kept close to me from the latter town to Stafford. My attendant left me with five miles to go to obtain accommodation for the night. A mile from the finish he met me again with the doleful news that no bath was to be had unless we cared to wait for an hour and-a-half. Whereupon the gentleman in the trap, before referred to, at once invited us to go with him to his place.

He turned out to be the proprietor of the Eagle Hotel. When he learned that we were vegetarians, he and his wife put themselves to a great deal of trouble to get us a variety of fruits and salads. I never wish to be better treated than I was that night.

I hate the drink traffic like poison, but that does not blind me to kindness of heart wherever I see it. Kindness is not confined to any cult or creed. I prefer the sins of this publican to the virtues of many people.

That night I slept peacefully, feeling I had

met a friend indeed, and also with the consolation afforded by reason of having exceeded my book by 6¼ miles.

It is worth mentioning that I walked from Penkridge to Stafford at the rate of 5¼ miles per hour.

ॐ ॐ

Eighth Day.—Tuesday, September 6th.

ॐ

Stafford to Manchester.—52½ Miles.
Total—379 Miles.

ॐ

I HAD now become eager to try and reach Manchester this day, and by 4 o'clock we had made a start. My mind was set upon Glasgow by Saturday.

Our friend, the publican, saw us off, and gave us full directions (no "*straight out*"), and without much difficulty we got clear of the town.

Stone, 7½ miles, was left slightly to the right. The roads were good with the exception of those around Newcastle-under-Lyne. At this place my cyclist had some trouble to get a breakfast, but eventually he succeeded in scrambling one together.

By 8.45 we had finished our meal and were off again.

The next town of any importance passed through was Congleton. The road winds very much through this place, and we were frequently obliged to enquire our way. The natives had heard of the walk and were out in full force.

The climb out of the town is rather stiff, then the surface of the road as far as Cheadle is perfect.

It is remarkable, on a tour of this description, what a lot of champion athletes one meets. True, they have never inscribed their names on the scroll of fame, but one might be led to believe, if their own account of themselves is to be taken as correct, that they are a species of athletic flower " born to blush unseen, and waste their sweetness on the desert air." Such an one I found this day. While plodding along some two miles beyond Congleton, a clatter of clogs just behind me caused me to glance round. There I espied an over-trained looking man, whose age may have been anything between 30 and 80 years. Along he came, with his arms up and swinging, in real racing style.

With a look of contempt at me, he told me I was going slow. When I gently reminded him that I had several hundreds of miles yet before me, while possibly he was going no further than the nearest wayside inn, or home to dinner, he paused a little, and then remarked that the pace I was then going at " would wear a few out in a day."

This man interested me very much. He reminded me of two clowns I once saw at a local circus, who rejoiced in the names of August and September, therefore I gave him a little encouragement, so to speak. What he had done, and what he could do together (chiefly the latter) made me feel small indeed. Forty-five to fifty miles a day would be for him a "sweet thing" he remarked. "Could I get him a job at walking from End-to-End ? "

When he found what an expensive luxury record-breaking was, his enthusiasm evaporated somewhat. By the way, I learned on closer enquiry that the farthest he had ever walked in a day was 30 miles. The self-confidence of some people is truly remarkable. Entering into the spirit of the whole thing, I suggested that he might have a try at swimming the

Channel, but he did not enthuse much about this, notwithstanding my reminder, that if he only succeeded in diving in and rounding the pier he would do about as well as some of the aspirants to the honour.

By this time beads of perspiration stood upon my friend's manly brow. The fact was I had increased my speed considerably, for the purpose of testing his powers. Duty or dinner now called him, and he left me rather abruptly, just before the Devenport Arms was reached, with a hearty "good luck to you."

My dinner here awaited me, the sublime, so to speak, after the ridiculous.

The scenery of Cheshire from Congleton to Cheadle is very pretty indeed. I wonder some company has not boomed it in these days, when everything from pills to piety is exploited for financial gain.

Ten miles before reaching Manchester, enthusiastic friends began to meet us; they all seemed delighted at my fresh appearance and springy step. When they heard that about two days had already been cut off the record and that I had hopes of reducing it by a more, they were overjoyed.

Tea and a good rest at Cheadle, then the
Lancashire sets were before me for forty miles.

By the time I reached Seedley, where I
stayed the night with a friend, both my heels
were blistered, and my feet were in a worse
condition than they had been from the start.

That night I had tea to drink with my supper.
It was the worst night's rest I had the whole of
the journey.   The thought of the blisters, and
the Lancashire sets the next morning was anything but cheering.   However, I was looked
after splendidly, which counts for much on a
walk like this.

That day I was 14 miles in excess of my
book distance.

Ninth Day.—Wednesday, Sept. 7th.

Manchester to Lancaster—53¼ Miles.
Total—432¼ Miles.

ANYTHING but a cheerful feeling
possessed me, when at 4 a.m. accompanied by my attendant and
Manchester friend, another day's work was
commenced.

Between my blistered feet and a cold driving rain, to say nothing of the shocking roads, the outlook was gloomy indeed.

Preston was originally fixed upon as the stopping place for the night, but I determined to try if possible to reach Lancaster, $21\frac{1}{4}$ miles beyond.

At Swinton and Bolton the mill hands were going to their daily toil. By the time Horwich was reached I was, to use an athletic term, decidedly "groggy," and my Manchester friend's face was wearing a very gloomy expression. There we had our first meal, and started out again in the rain.

By the time we had reached Chorley (23 miles) the rain had ceased, but my feet were worse than ever. At Preston we had dinner. Just previous to this, one of the blisters had burst, but the other pained me very much.

For those who have never enjoyed the doubtful pleasure of walking with blistered feet, allow me to introduce you to an experience which once having gone through you will never forget. This is what happens :—

Unconsciously at first your feet begin to blister. Your first intimation of the fact comes to you, perhaps, from stepping on a stone, or a slight twist on a rough part of the road. Presently the blister bursts, and for a minute or two the agony is excruciating. Then all pain leaves for a time. If the blood is in good condition, and if you have sufficiently trained your feet, so that they are able to bear the strain put upon them, they will from this time harden ; but woe be to you, if you are wanting in physical fitness, for, first inflamma‑tion, and then festering, sets in, the end theu is only a question of time.

When I started from Preston, after dinner, I went with a decided limp. My Manchester friend left us here looking very sad. I did not know then what the load on his mind was—I know now.

He had been with me during the worst time I had on the whole journey with my feet.

Now we had a splendid stretch of road be‑fore us to Lancaster. By the time the "Hamilton Arms" was reached at 5.25, and tea had been partaken of, my feet had healed and I felt like a giant refreshed.

Any fears that may have been entertained regarding my feet now vanished, for we knew the worst was over, now that the sets were left behind.

" Harmers" Temperance Hotel, Lancaster, was entered at 8.15 p.m., and by 9.15, both my attendant and myself were fast asleep.

✻ ✻

Tenth Day.—Thursday, Sept. 8th.

✻

Lancaster to Penrith—47½Miles.
Total—479¾ Miles.

✻

WE made a rather late start to-day. I had intended it should be so. In view of the trying day before us, it was policy to get a good night's rest.

By 5 o'clock, however, we were threading our way in the semi-darkness through the streets of Lancaster. The pavements were very slippy, for it was again raining, and I did not feel a bit glad.

A mist hung over Morecambe Bay as we passed, and the smoking furnaces of the iron-works at Carnforth (6½ miles) were a blot on the landscape.

About this time the rain abated and the day

looked more promising.. We had our breakfast at a wayside inn, 18 miles from Lancaster,
and braced ourselves up for the Shap Fell.

By the time Kendal was reached, at 11.30,
the rain had again resumed business, a gloomy
outlook indeed for us ; but he who attempts a
record of this description must rise superior to
all climatic conditions, or give up.

At this town the people watched us eagerly
as we passed ; some walked a short distance
with us, in silence. The weather has more to
do with our moods than some of us care to
admit.

Climbing the Shap Fell.

Kendal had scarcely been left behind when
the ascent of the Shap Fell commenced.

Once previously, I had walked across on a
very hot day. I thought then that no weather
could be worse than that. I had yet to have
the present experience. Dreary, indeed, was
the outlook. The road at first was fair ; but
the farther we got, the worse it became, until
it was shocking. The elements, also, for a
time seemed to be conspiring to break me up.

One mistake had been made at the outset of
this week. I had sent my sweater on in the

portmanteau to Glasgow, thinking that I should not require it before the Grampians were reached, and I had to pay the penalty.

Here I was, with nothing but a light alpaca coat, and thin athletic jersey between my body and the elements. Every minute the air became colder and colder as we advanced, and the storm was gaining in fury.

The workmen engaged in laying the underground cable here gave a word or two of encouragement, and asked me how I felt. I could not very truthfully say I was enjoying it, for, to be perfectly candid, I was feeling very miserable. And now the milestone on our right read—6 miles to Kendal; 10 miles to Shap.

We enquired of a workman how far it was to the summit, and he replied " several miles."

What an outlook !

Yet press on we must, or give up the idea of reaching Penrith that night, and Glasgow by the week end. The weather was having a bad effect on my cycling friend ; still he kept close to me faithfully, notwithstanding that he was soaked through, waterproof (?) cape and all.

How keenly we looked (as well as the blind
ing rain would allow) for each milestone.

Another stone !—No ; it was a piece of rock,
which in our eagerness had been mistaken for
a milestone. Some three hundred yards or so
farther we read—9 miles to Kendal ; 7 miles
to Shap.

We seemed to have left the former town an
age, but after consulting the watch my cyclist
informed me that it was now 1.45 p.m. I had
covered thus nine miles at the rate of just four
miles per hour.

A little later we reached the summit. My
hands were numbed with the cold, and it required a great effort to keep going.

When the next stone told 6 miles to Shap,
I thought it advisable to let my friend go and
order a meal at the village, and giving him instructions where to make for, I was left alone
on the cold hillside.

The road was now vile, extremely uneven,
with quantities of loose road metal about,
which made firm foothold impossible. Ever
and anon the explosion of the blasting charges
at the quarries hard by, seemed to increase the
dullness of things. I fell to wondering how it

must be to get lost on the mountains in winter, and tried to take my mind off my present miseries by various means, but all seemed a failure; I was getting more downcast every minute.

Five miles to Shap; eleven to Kendal. Another hour-and-a-quarter and I should be snug.

Hark! What is that?

Passing a wayside cottage, the home evidently of one of the quarrymen, the music of a piano (much out of tune) greeted me. A little nearer, and the tune of a favourite hymn seemed to be coming from a higher world. It may have been a bad attempt by a very bad musician, but the grandest music of the gods could not have been more cheering to me; most of my misery vanished, and I went on my way very much braced up.

Three miles to Shap!

I encouraged myself with the thought that in about 45 minutes I should be getting ready for dinner. Away I plodded. The sight of the village, and the beaming countenance of Mr. Tom. Conchie, the guide and mountain-racer, met me. When his house was reached,

there sat my friend the cyclist, arrayed in a
pair of trousers several sizes too large for him,
anxiously awaiting me.

I was very cold and rather miserable, but a
suit of dry clothes and a good rub down
worked wonders, and by the time dinner was
served I was myself again, and looking eagerly
forward to making another start.

Time of arrival at Shap village, 3.30 p.m.

I had covered the 16¼ miles from Kendal in
exactly four hours, a good bit of walking, all
things considered.

By 4.45 we were once more under way The
storm had cleared, and Old Sol was beaming
cheerfully upon us. I was feeling in splendid
condition, notwithstanding what I had lately
passed through, and by 7.15 Penrith was made.

We entered the town accompanied by a few
enthusiasts. By arriving there about half-a-day
sooner than we were expected, we missed the
crowd, which invariably turns out to greet all
record-breakers passing through.

At the Exchange Temperance Hotel we
were treated right royally, and by 9.30 were
snugly in bed, with 113 miles before us for the
next two days.   .

Eleventh Day.—Friday, Sept. 9th.

Penrith to Beattock—56¾ Miles. Total—536¼ Miles.

ON this morning the record for early rising was beaten; before 4 a.m. we were on our way for Carlisle, where we intended having breakfast.

When we left our hotel it was quite dark. At a junction of roads a friendly policeman directed us and saved us from going the wrong way. The morning was clear, but the sun was a little too bright early on to suit me : I thought it foretold a wet day, and so it did.

Our breakfast at Carlisle (18 miles) was enjoyed very much, after which we set out for Scotland, where we arrived, eight miles further on.

The border was crossed at 11.40 a.m. The old lady at the toll bar (the first house in Scotland) signed our book. This is the house famous for so many marriages of run-away couples having been solemnised here.

A strong wind was now blowing directly in our faces which made walking and cycling

difficult.   On one occasion a sudden gust of
wind blew my friend over.   The Solway Firth,
on our right, looked very rough, and the
village of Gretna Green wore a deserted look
as we passed through.

Already the houses began to have a Scotch
appearance ; the brogue had also altered considerably.   We had scarcely left Gretna Green
behind when the rain commenced.   Five miles
from Ecclefechan my friend left me to order
the mid-day meal.

At the Bush Hotel, Ecclefechan (36¼ miles),
we stayed for dinner.   A plain stone slab, on a
very plain house opposite, informed us that—
" In this house Thomas Carlyle was born."
Why he left Ecclefechan for Chelsea passes my
comprehension I must admit.   I wonder how
many times he yearned for the country life.
He may have been thinking of his home
when he wrote that immortal part of " Sartor
Resartus " commencing " Two men I honour
and no third."

After dinner and a shave, the latter being a
luxury I had not indulged in that week, so
intent had I been upon the walk, we started
for Beattock at 3.30 p.m.

At St. Mungo we called on some friends but could only afford a few minutes delay.

By the time we reached Locherbie ($14\frac{1}{2}$ miles before Beattock) the rain was pouring down and the out-look was grim. Hereabouts the country wears a rather bleak appearance ; especially did it to-day in the rain. We were having a second edition of yesterday's experience ; but on this occasion it did not affect me nearly so much.

I consoled my cyclist by telling him that we would be all right once Glasgow was reached ; kind friends would be ready to help us there. With about six or seven miles to go, he left me to arrange accommodation for the night.

I gave him instructions where to apply first, and if that failed, he was to do his best ; in any case he was to leave his bicycle alight outside the place we were to stay at. With that he left me alone, with the bleak, bare country for company. It was not enjoyable, but I told myself of the feeling of satisfaction which would be mine once it was finished.

My cyclist kept up his spirits well, considering. Personally, I felt rather tired when he left me. Thoughts of home and the dear ones there eager for my success relieved the monotony somewhat.

It was now quite dark. I had no means of judging the distance, as I had not a watch, so I kept going forward at a good pace—the only thing to do under the circumstances.

When the village was entered I kept a sharp look-out for the bicycle light and was soon rewarded by seeing its welcome gleam.

In another minute I was safely inside a cheerful room, with a good fire to comfort me.

My friend was arrayed in a dry borrowed suit of fearful and wonderful cut and colour.

While he was attending me in the bath, he told how he had been to the door several times and called my name, so anxious had he been about me.

A large plate of toast (a favourite delicacy of mine) and some cheese and salad repaired my flagging energies. While we were enjoying this meal, my cyclist friend enquired what time I intended leaving on the morrow. and whether I should make an early start if the rain continued. I told him to let to-morrow take care of itself ; it would be bad enough if we had to climb the Beattock Mountain under unfavourable conditions when it came, without thinking of it now. At present, rest for the night was our chief concern. With these thoughts, and many others, we retired as quicky as possible.

If my friend had any fears about the weather they were groundless, as we sha l see presently.

*   *

Twelfth Day.—Saturday, Sept. 10th.

*

Beattock to Glasgow,—56¼ Miles. Total—593 Miles.

*

DURING the night the storm had cleared away, so that when we made a start for the day at 5.15 a.m., the stars were shining brightly in the clear sky. Just a nip of frost in the air made the morning rather cold—a little too much so. Taken all round, it was far better than we had expected from the promise of last night.

The week seemed already at an end. No pause was made until 20 miles had been left behind, then the breakfast at Abington was discussed.

During the early hours of the morning my friend dismounted several times to get a signature and sometimes to walk with me, beating his hands to keep up the circulation.

The road from Beattock village to Abington crosses the summit of Beattock Mountain, 1,025 feet above sea level.

The scenery may be described as ordinary, for it consists nearly entirely of wild moorland. Still it has a grandeur all its own, and we enjoyed it.

We were both glad when after breakfast the time came for moving, for we had not enjoyed this meal very much.

Another 36 miles and Glasgow would be reached, and the record week's work ended.

My attendant tried in vain to get a meal at Blackwood, $9\frac{1}{2}$ miles past Lesmahagow, but was compelled to push on to Larkhall for it.

About this time friends from Hamilton, Glasgow, Larkhall, etc., were meeting us. Their company was very welcome.

We had a good meal at a friend's house at Larkhall where we stayed $1\frac{1}{2}$ hours.

It was a triumphal procession from here to Glasgow. Quite a crowd walked or rode all the way. Long before we arrived in town the news had got abroad consequent upon an announcement in the *Glasgow Evening News* that I might be expected between nine and ten o'clock.

I dislike crowds; the contrast from my quiet country life is too much, and to-night it was a specially large one. However, the Royal Exchange was reached in safety.

Had I paused only a few seconds I should have been hemmed in, with the possibility of having my feet damaged, but a tram car just starting was utilised to stop the crowd. We jumped in and were off.

A mental review of the week, as the tram moved along, was very satisfactory.

I had covered 320 miles in the last six days (47 more than the previous week) and had an average of 53 miles per day.

My physical condition was good, except that I had a rather bad blister on my right heel, and that I was feeling the effects of the very crude feeding arrangements which had obtained since Worcester. How the latter defect was remedied, to-morrow must tell.

Sunday, September 11th.

T HE record week of the walk had been one of anxiety in many ways. To walk 320 miles with the absence of any proper arrangement for food was anything but satisfactory. My attendant had done his best, and done it well, but he was human, and could not be expected to do two or three men's work.

Other record-breakers generally get attended by quite a small army of pace-makers, etc., to say nothing of a motor-car to carry necessary clothing, food, and other essentials. The path of reform is always hard, and rightly so. The earnest ones only keep to it, for any length of time. It did not matter so much the first week when only 273 miles were covered ; but it was a different problem with 47 miles added to the distance.

We had the choice of two evils.

My attendant had to be away from me about the half of each day ordering meals, or we must make shift with what happened to be going. I preferred to lose a little in nutriment and have the company of my friend more ; for it is terribly monotonous, on a walk like this, jogging away alone for hours, especially in deserted parts of the country.

White bread and eggs with fruit and salads, when obtainable, were our chief food from Worcester to Glasgow, consequently in the absence of green vegetables I arrived at the latter town rather *hungry*.

My vegetable dinners were missed very much.

Before retiring to rest on Saturday, and immediately after a warm bath, I ate a good meal of cooked cheese, and on Sunday I had five good square meals. Indeed, I kept the good lady of the house where I stayed a good part of the day looking after my food. It was a real surprise for her.

I had either to start on Monday with a low store of vitality, or eat sufficient food to enable me to make it up and risk the possibility of overtaxing my stomach. I chose the latter course, and beyond a slight internal looseness, I felt no ill effects, thanks to my powers of assimilation.

The offer by the Scottish Vegetarian Society of two men to accompany me for the remainder of the walk, was gladly accepted by me.

To start with on Monday, I had now my English friend and a Scotchman, both cyclists, and another to go forward each day by train, to order the mid-day meal and accommodation for the night,—a kind of advance agent, in fact.

The clouds had now cleared. By 9 o'clock I was snug in bed, feeling that all difficulties had vanished, and looking eagerly forward to the following day, decided in my mind to make an attempt to finish the walk before another Sunday ; but I never once expected to do what 1 did.

Thirteenth Day.—Monday, Sept. 12th.

Glasgow to Perth—60½ Miles.
Total—653½ Miles.

BY 5 o'clock this morning a fair sized crowd of vegetarian and other enthusiasts had collected in front of the Royal Exchange to give me a hearty send-off. Punctually on the stroke of the hour I went away.

My action was not too encouraging to an onlooker. I was feeling rather stiff, one always does after a day's rest following a hard week's walking.

In spite of this I felt very strong, and decided to try and get to Earn Bridge (53 miles) that day.

The breakfast at Cumbernauld was splendid. By the time I had got fairly going again, the stiffness that held me at the start had worn off, and I improved as the day advanced. The dinner at Bridge-of-Allan (30 miles), provided by a kind lady vegetarian friend, was excellent. I shall never forget the look our kind hostess gave me at parting. She was wondering how I should fare later. In answer to her enquiry as to how I felt, and what I thought would be the result, I assured her that there was nothing to be alarmed at in any way, and that it was not now a question of beating the *record*, but *how much* I should beat it by.

With many wishes for my success, we left here at 2 o'clock, after a stay of 70 minutes.

A friend had walked with me from Glasgow to this place; he now returned after a hearty hand shake.

I had almost forgotten to mention that just
before entering Stirling 3½ miles from Bridge-
of-Allan) I noticed a sign-board directing to
the field of Bannockburn.

The Wallace Memorial, just outside the
town, looked majestic in the sunlight.

Auchterarder was our next stopping-place.
Here we had a good tea, and enquired respect-
ing hotel accommodation at Earn Bridge, and
found that such a thing did not exist there, and
were told that in all probability we should be
obliged to go as far as Perth for a decent place
for the night.   Ever since dinner time I had
cherished a secret longing that we should be
obliged to go to Perth that night, and it happened just as I wanted it.   The fates seemed
to be favouring me.

By the time Earn Bridge was reached it was
quite dark.   Our advance agent met us with
the news that if I wanted to stay here I should
be forced to put up with very unsuitable accommodation and without a bath.

Would I go to Perth ?

Did I feel equal to it ?

Not only did I feel equal but my heart fairly
leaped within me at the prospect ; for I

reckoned that by reaching Perth that night, a 17½ days performance was made possible, if all went well.

My agent friend gladly shouldered the portmanteau and followed me. By 9.45 p.m. we had reached our hotel, and by 11 were asleep in bed, at any rate I was, with my mind set on reaching Dalwhinnie on the morrow.

✦ ✦

Fourteenth Day.—Tuesday, Sept. 13th.

✦

Perth to Dalwhinnie.—57¾ Miles.

Total—711¼ Miles.

✦

AT five o'clock sharp another start was made. We had some difficulty in finding our way out of the town, but eventually we got safely on to the high road, and all was well.

For the first few miles the scenery was decidedly plain, but after Bankfoot is passed (8¾ miles) it improves and a little distance before Dunkeld is reached it becomes splendid.

Birnam Hill and Wood, immortalised by

Shakespere in his "Macbeth," looked charming, notwithstanding the rain that was now falling. The clouds drifting around the hill and wood brought up thoughts of the three wierd sisters and their magic pot. A native informed me that the spot where Macbeth was supposed to have met them was close by.

At Dunkeld ($14\frac{3}{4}$ miles) we had breakfast. There was no time to spare for drying wet clothes ; we were getting more interested in the walk and did not want to jeopardise the time by long rests. A good story was heard here about a certain record-breaker and his food, but we must not repeat it.

At Ballinlugg the sun came out. The morning rain had refreshed the landscape. Another five miles and Pitlochry was reached, Here we saw a man in kilts for the first time since starting on the walk. He was not a good physical specimen. He ought to have worn trousers. Why, ah, why, do men with spindle shanks wear kilts or knickerbockers ?

Mounted stags heads, marked at two guineas each, were displayed in front of a shop, presumably for men of a sporting turn of mind, to carry home as trophies of the chase !

From Pitlochry to Blair Athol the scenery defies description—it has to been seen to be understood. The pretty waterfalls and glens hereabouts, comprise the finest scenery I have ever witnessed.

We had left our English cyclist in Dunkeld, having his machine repaired. He came on by train and so missed this scenery.

The Pass of Killiecrankie brought back memories of stirring times, when manly power was reckoned by strength of muscle and will. To-day we do things rather differently, but perhaps not much better, when we take money as a standard of worth. Power is often a question of craft and greed.

We had been advised to go to the Tilt Hotel, Blair Athol, for dinner, and thither we repaired. By this time we were all together again, the three attendants and myself.

The damaged cycle had been put right, and my friend met us about half-a-mile before Blair Athole was reached.

The dinner, like the scenery, was splendid. The host spared no pains to do his best for us, and provided a varied and nutritious meal, and when we left he refused to take any

E

money, preferring to make us a present of it in consideration of the handsome way we were beating the record.

A guide-book was consulted for information regarding Dalwhinnie. This place was described as a bleak, desolate spot, protected by a few fir trees : a not very cheering piece of news after the fine scenery of the morning.

Leaving Blair Athol, we commenced

CROSSING THE GRAMPIAN MOUNTAINS.

As we ascended, the landscape became more bleak and bare, so that by the time we had put 40 miles for the day behind our backs, about the only redeeming feature was the river Garry, along the banks of which the road and railway run for miles.

In many places the river runs down pretty waterfalls or rapids.

I was now left one cyclist only. Where the other one had gone to we knew not. The last time we saw him, we remembered noticing his vigorous efforts to inflate a tyre, and so we concluded that he was troubled with a puncture. The unfortunate part was, he had our knapsack with him containing, amongst other things, the emergency rations.

When we heard at Dalnacardock, a village of one or two houses, that there was no accommodation for food until Dalwhinnie was reached, we were sorely troubled. This meant that I should be obliged to walk $23\frac{1}{2}$ miles between my dinner and tea, a rather risky proceeding, to go so far, considering the tremendous daily distances we were covering.

The road had now become very rough and rather steep. In places it was overgrown with grass, and we were 1.000 feet above sea level. The bracing air had a most invigorating effect upon me, which also means that I was getting hungry. About three miles later my single attendant left me to try to get a meal. He was instructed to go to the first house he saw, and place our difficulty before whoever opened to him, then I felt certain he would obtain all that was necessary.

Scarcely had he left me when I saw someone wildly gesticulating from the window of a railway carriage in a passing train. It was our friend the advance man. He also had emergency rations with him in the portmanteau.

When my cyclist saw the train, about $1\frac{1}{2}$

miles further on, he made a dash for Dalnaspidal railway station, and fetched our friend
out of the train with the bag.

It was the work of a very few minutes to go
to the adjoining house, place our needs before
the good lady, and her kindly daughter. A
meal was hastily prepared, and by the time I
arrived it was nearly ready.

Here my one dietetic weakness had full play.
The daughter of the house very generously
toasted bread and buttered it as fast as I could
consume it.

I felt at home with quite a large family
of children of varying ages seated about.
When, all too soon, the time for departure
came, we were sorry to leave. With a last
look at Loch Garry from the window of the
house, we left after a stay of about an hour.

A quarter of an hour later the highest part
of the road across the Grampians was reached
and six miles yet remained to be covered
before the day's work was ended.

Our cyclist pushed on as well as he could
over the rough road, to make our accommodation for the night certain. He had two spills,
besides being nearly run down by a motor car

without a light.

The cyclist we had left behind had not shown up yet, and we were feeling a little anxious about him.

The friend with the portmanteau and myself stumbled and walked along in the darkness as well as the looseness of the roads would allow, my feet suffering somewhat in the process. At 9.5 p.m. the Loch Erith Hotel, Dalwhinnie was reached, and another day accounted for.

We were all comfortably seated at the supper table when a scared face looked in at the window. It was our Scotch cyclist. His machine had broken down and he had been obliged to walk the whole distance since we last saw him.

We all felt relieved when he came in, none the worse for his experience.

Dr. Deighton had stayed here a night. He had taken three days to walk from Glasgow— I had covered the distance in two.

Fifteenth Day.—Wednesday, Sept. 14th.

*

Dalwhinnie to Inverness—59¼ Miles.
Total—770½ Miles.

*

THE air was clear and frosty when at 5 o'clock we made a start for the day. For the first time it was found necessary to don sweater and gloves, and to now and again beat my hands across my chest to keep up a vigorous circulation.

How we enjoyed this morning to Kingussie. The descent of the mountain was just gradual enough to be of assistance without shaking one.

An athlete, in running costume, enjoying an early morning spin was passed near Newtonmore. The road was improving also, and by the time Kingussie was reached it was in grand condition. The Grampian Mountains were now behind us, and we had a good meal here.

Whilst we were enjoying this meal I felt as if I was being instilled with a new lease of life. Cyclist No. 2 now came up. He had been in bed a little longer on this morning, after his experience of the day before, and we all had our meal together.

An idea of trying for 17 days here entered my mind. When I told my two attendants of this, they both urged me to go for it by all means, if I felt fit, and so it was decided that if Inverness was reached that night, and I was in good condition, we would try to beat the record by $7\frac{1}{4}$ days.

I now worked with this object in view.

Twelve miles further, Loch Aviemore on our right looked splendid, for now the weather was perfect, and we all felt it was good to be living upon this beautiful earth.

At Carrbridge ($34\frac{3}{4}$ miles from Dalwhinnie) we had a splendid spread; but after a good meal and an hour's stay I came out of the hotel in an exhausted condition, and thereby hangs a tale.

Ever since the commencement of the walk, I had insisted on taking my meals in a private room whenever possible. To-day dinner was served in a public dining-room. The feeling of strength flowing into me, when all is quiet, was absent here with so many people about, and I was very glad to leave after a stay of an hour.

The road from here to Inverness was undula-
tng and loose.

By the time Craggie Inn (52 miles for the
day) was reached, I was feeling low-spirited
and tired.   A rest and a meal were taken. We
had some fine wholemeal bread in this out-of-
the-way inn.   This, with the salads, and 40
minutes rest, worked wonders, and the last $7\frac{1}{4}$
miles was done rather easily.

The news of my progress had preceded me,
and the small boy was very much in evidence,
as we entered the town.   The language at this
place is very clear and musical : it was pleasing
to listen to.

M·Gilvray's Temperance Hotel was entered
by 40 minutes past nine.

While in the bath I was astonished at the
hardness of the soap.   After a futile attempt
to get a lather, I found I had been using the
bathbrick.

Another 140 miles and all would be over.
I determined now to try to cover this inside
two days.

Sixteenth Day.—Thursday, Sept. 15th.

*

Inverness to Golspie—65¾ Miles.
Total—836¼ Miles.

*

WE did not spend overmuch time in sleep, for by 4.40 a.m. we were on our way once more. The morning was just beginning to dawn as we left the town. Inverness Castle, on our left, looked weird in the dim light.

Workmen were met occasionally going slowly to their daiiy toil. Corn in stooks was everywhere to be seen, for the harvest was in full swing.

The rough roads of the Grampians hae played havoc with my feet, for at this timd they were very sore and weary; but by the time we had reached Beauley (famous for its priory) that feeling began to wear off. We had now walked 12½ miles, mostly by the sea coast. We had been going directly west, to get round the Moray Firth; but here a sharp turn of the road for the north brought us once more direct for John o' Groat's.

We had breakfast at Muir of Ord, 2½ miles
further. The rest of 55 minutes picked me
up splendidly, and I felt quite myself, once I
had got fairly into the swing, after this meal.
Again we were walking by the sea shore. The
Black Isle was in view all the morning, in fact
until Alness was reached.

Conan was left behind, so was the old town
of Dingwall, and dinner was obtained at a
wayside inn at Kilday. There we arrived
3.40 p.m., having walked 26½ miles since the
last meal, and 40 miles that day. I could only
spare 50 minutes at this point, and then we
were off for Mickle Ferry. That must be
reached before dusk, or it might mean a stay
for the night on this side and that would be a
serious matter for the record.

At last, Tain (46 miles) was reached, It was
early-closing day for the shops. One of my
cyclists tried in vain to get some raisins, while
the other went forward to signal the ferry,
Leaving this neat town of Tain a sharp-looking
boy on a bicycle pioneered me to the ferry in
the absence of my cyclists. I was glad of his
company : it helped to while the time away.
His name, Rory M'Tavish, was as thoroughly

Scotch as he was himself.

Two or three miles before the ferry was reached, I could discern the white sails of the boat coming across. This, I thought, was all right, but a little later, when I saw it returning to the north side, my spirits dropped a little. It was a very short stay which it made the *s* before it again came to the side we were on.

Again my spirits arose.

By the time I had reached the landing-stage I was able to step without the slightest delay into the boat with the two cyclists, and we were sailing across in the calm twilight of a peaceful evening. The waters washing the sides of the boat seemed to be inviting me to be lulled to sleep. I strove against this inclination, for Golspie was yet 15 miles ahead.

The inability to obtain the food we wanted necessitated a stop for a meal at Clashmore ($53\frac{1}{2}$ miles).

Accommodation for this was obtained at a baker's shop in the village.

An old lady, with a kind, honest face, looked after our creature comforts, and left her ironing to do so. We heard some news of previous record-breakers who had stayed here.

Very high in the opinion of our hostess stood Miss Rosa Symonds, our own champion lady cyclist, who makes a short stay here each time she comes this way.

I had begrudged this stop, but was glad to meet such a fine character as this woman in such an out-of-the-way spot, and would not have considered a much longer delay as time wasted. As I left the house she shook my hand warmly, and spoke to me with a touch of deep affection in her voice. Her parting words are too sacred to bring out here to the public gaze, but I shall never forget them as long as I live.

What an experience I was having. I was glad we were in the dark, or my two friends may have thought me a very weak man.

All was silent: the distance was telling upon us.

The English attendant now left us and went forward to Golspie, where our advance man was anxiously awaiting us.

The day had been an exciting one, and we all knew he would be uneasy until we arrived.

By a rather circuitous route we safely negotiated Mound Station and a few miles later heard the stentorian voice of our friend ahead of us. Cheerfully we responded, and two or three minutes later, he was running to meet us in his eagerness, enquiring in a hushed voice how I felt.

I answered him that all was well ; besides which my easy action indicated my fit condition.

Though the hour was late several local enthusiasts were waiting to see me arrive.

Our friend beguiled the next quarter of an hour by telling how he had succeeded in getting the night's accommodation.

At first the landlady of the Témperance Hotel refused to entertain the idea of putting me up, when she heard what I was engaged in, " for" said she " I don't want him to die on my hands."

My friend's "Y.M.C.A." card of membership did the trick, however, and when I arrived she looked closely at me, ane then exclaimed, " Oh ! he's all right."

How strange ; some people will look at any character, rather than the one we all carry with us.

By the time we arrived at Golspie it was

12.15, and we had another 73½ miles yet to walk.

The cyclists gave every sign of wearying, and it was decided, in view of the heavy day to follow, that one should stay in bed a little longer on the morrow, to make certain that some one should be with me at the finish. To bed and sleep. I felt it was needed.

≫ ≫

Seventeenth Day.—Friday, Sept. 16th.

≫

Golspie to John o' Groat's—73½ Miles. Total—909¾ Miles.

≫

AFTER less than four hours sleep, I awoke on this last morning of the walk, feeling somewhat reluctant to rise, and no wonder, after such a heavy week. However, this was quickly shaken off, and by 6 o'clock we were on our way for John o' Groat's.

All the humour was very grim with 73½ miles facing us. We felt that a responsibility was resting upon us. Now that the task was so near completion the mental strain was increasing every minute.

One of the party voiced his feelings by saying that "If we did not finish quickly, we should all be in a lunatic asylum." The laugh that followed did us all good.

Dunrobin Castle, on the right, about a mile out of Golspie, looked imposing. This is the seat of the Duke of Sutherland. There we were told by a carter, who signed our book, that we had passed the residence of Mr. Andrew Carnegie the night previous.

By the time Brora (6 miles) was reached the feeling of weariness that possessed me at the start of the morning had begun to wear off.

The waves beating on the shore seemed to speak of rest just ahead, and stimulated me to fresh effort.

By the time Helmsdale ($17\frac{1}{2}$ miles) was made, I was quite ready for the breakfast awaiting me there.

A telegram was sent from this point to the hotel at John o' Groat's asking them to be expecting us about 2.30 the following morning.

When we left, one of the party was doing a little propaganda with a small group of natives around him listening to his earnest appeal for vegetarianism.

Now we were crossing the Ord of Caithness, a wild, mountainous stretch, consisting mainly of moorland, used for shooting purposes. When we saw the look of gentle trustfulness in the eyes of the deer we wondered how anyone could find in their heart to shoot them in cold blood.

In a very exposed part of the Ord we saw a white tombstone bearing the following inscription : " On this spot perished William Welch," then followed the date, which I forget. Enquiring from a shepherd as to what this meant, he told us that William Welch was a wandering tramp who was found dead on that spot after a very cold night. He had left this world for the better land he was so fond of talking about, and so great was the loss felt, that the people round about had erected this simple stone as a declaration of their love for him.

The story was very touching. In my imagination the blanks were filled in. I thought of him, dying all alone ; beaten by the cold ; yet not alone, for the One who gave His life to bless the earth was now taking him lovingly to his reward ; and then I thought of another Tramp in Gallilee, one who walked 50 miles out and 50 back again to see a poor sick girl.; and then began to wonder how long it would be before people would begin to realise that the only life which can be called life is to be in harmony with our own consciences. That life lived well, is a life of usefulness and joy, be it lived by a tramp or a king. Any other life is death, no matter what the world says.

These thoughts, and many more, ran through my mind as we crossed this barren land.

The roads were not of the best by any means, the sudden drop at Berridale being the worst of all. Another rather steep bit of road at Dunbeath (famous for its castle) did not help us in any way.

The monotony, occasioned largely by the almost treeless condition of the landscape, was relieved somewhat by the majestic cliffs and the sea on our right.

After leaving Brora, we never lost sight of the coast for very long all the way to the finish.

At Latheron Wheel Hotel we had our dinner. When I came out again I felt very fresh, but this feeling soon wore off. The

F

walk was telling on me, as may be expected.

Our next pause, and last, was to be at Wick. Thither our advance agent had gone from Helmsdale to prepare a good meal to stay us during the last stage of the walk.

At the hotel a call for salads was responded to by an enquiry " whether a raw cabbage would be suitable ? "

Long before Wick was reached my eagerness was very apparent to my cyclists. When one of them kept falling slightly intt the rear, I requested him rather sharply to leave me alone, go to Wick, and get the others ready.

At last this town was reached, and a good reception awaited me. The doors of the Railway Hotel were beseiged by the natives while we were having our meal.

After staying here 45 minutes, I was off again.

I seemed quite fresh, for I moved along freely and strong, but this wore off very soon.

By the time Wick had been left four miles behind, those who had started to walk with us to the finish had all fallen out, and we were left with ourselves. All the party was walking, the bicycles having been left at the hotel at Wick.

A milestone on our right, shining in the darkness, told eight miles to Wick. All except myself imagined that we had gone a mile further; a certain sign that we were longing for the end.

I was glad that my friends were all walking, they would now understand more about the task. The milestones were like beacon lights to us, and when one read half-a-mile to John o' Groat's, we all felt glad indeed.

" Now it *is* all over " whispered one. "Now it is *not* " said I " until we knock at the hotel door. It is possible, even yet, to sprain my ankle on this rough road."

A light on our left caused us all to exclaim —"there it is ! " We soon found that we were mistaken, for it was an ordinary cottage with a light inside. The sleeper within was aroused, and the information elicited that our destination lay along by the sea shore, about a quarter of a mile ahead.

I could have declared that we had gone at least half-a-mile from the last stone, such was my eagerness.

After what appeared a fairly good distance for a quarter of a mile, a light was seen on our right, and this, we all said, must be the hotel, and we were not mistaken this time.

By a winding road the door was reached.

A rather loud summons to open, a short wait, a rustle of skirts, and we were admitted by the proprietress, who was waiting up for us.

How glad I was to reach the end. I had enjoyed the walk, although it had its times of hardship and sometimes misery : what task worth doing has not ?

The clock facing us on entering told 2.33 a.m. The greatest athletic feat I had ever accomplished was concluded in 16 days, 21 hours, 33 minutes ; and my other partial failures were more than made up for.

A hot bath, a good meal, and I retired to take a well-earned rest, with a card bearing these words facing me :—

" *They that wait upon the Lord,*
shall renew their strength."

Photo. taken at finish of the walk.

Attendants:

1. - J. McNiel, Glasgow. 2. - J. Elder, Glasgow.
3. - J. Brinton, Birmingham.

Review of the Walk.

WEATHER.

TAKEN on the whole the weather conditions during the walk may be classed as average.

The first week was far too hot for comfort; the second was too wet; but I much prefer wet weather to hot, providing I had proper attention—say a motor car carrying a few suits of clothes and necessary small items, so that a change could be made as often as required; then I would not mind the rain. It is very discouraging to sit in wet clothing clothing while partaking of a meal.

The last week was perfect. If the elements had been ordered especially for us we could not have had better conditions. Just sun enough to cheer us but not enough to make the air and roads uncomfortable. The gentle breezes gave an added charm to the other favourable elements, which had much to do with the long distances covered during the final week.

FOOD.

A S this is a very important item in the eyes of many in a walk of this description, a list of food taken during the last week will be interesting.

I am giving the last week's menu, because it was by far the best, and I prefer to give the most nutritious week's food, so that people may not be misled; but here let me state, that I do not necessarily say that all people would be able to undergo such a physical and mental strain on such dietary. The other conditions of life under which they live differ so much from mine.

I live in the open air, six miles from the nearest town, and in the bracing air of the Cotswold Hills. This is a great factor in the food question. Our state of life is of far more importance than what we eat, and our attitude of mind of still greater importance as a factor in health, but lest I should be misunderstood, let me here say, that to give the impression that flesh foods are in any single case necessary for the purpose of sustaining the body in the finest physical condition is, in my opinion, not only misleading, but a statement based upon ignorance.

Then, again, it will be noticed that no manufactured concentrated food of any description was included in my list, another important item.

What I may have thought in the past need not be discussed ; but it is what I think now that is to me of vital importance.   My opinion, based upon practical experience is that all the food necessary for maintaining us in full enjoyment of health and strength can be selected from the *natural* world, without going to manufactured foods, even if they are vegetarian preparations.   Some of them may be convenient but never essential.

The physical future of the nation depends largely upon whether we are to be fed from the fields and orchards, or the factories and slaughter houses.   In the former lies the solution of many knotty social problems.

List of Foods Eaten During Last Week of Walk.

MONDAY.

1st meal :—Poached eggs on toast, lettuce, weak tea.

2nd meal :—Rissoles, cauliflower, potatoes, plum pudding, apple.

3rd meal :—White bread and butter, weak tea, biscuits.

Cup of coffee and two slices of white bread and butter just previous to retiring for the night. Walked 14½ miles before first meal.

TUESDAY.

1st meal :—Poached eggs on toast, weak tea.

2nd meal:—Cauliflower, potatoes, rice pudding, stewed fruit, tinned pears.

3rd meal :—White bread toasted (with butter), weak tea.

(I have an idea that here I had a little meatose (vegetarian food) with my friends, but if I did it was not more than an ounce or two.)

Cup of cocoa and white bread and butter just previous to retiring.

Walked 14½ miles before first meal.

WEDNESDAY.

1st meal :—Poached eggs on toast, weak tea.

2nd meal :—Potatoes, greens, white bread and cheese, rice pudding, with stewed plums.

3rd meal :—Wholemeal bread and butter, lettuce, weak tea.

Cup of cocoa, white bread and butter, and slice of melon just before going to bed.

Walked 18 miles before first meal.

⚜

THURSDAY.

1st meal:—Poached eggs on toast, white bread and butter, cheese, weak tea.

2nd meal :—Potatoes, greens, tinned pears, biscuits, weak tea.

3rd meal :—White bread and butter, cheese, weak tea.

Cup of cocoa and white bread and butter before retiring for the night.

Walked 15 miles before first meal.

⚜

FRIDAY.

1st meal :—Poached eggs on toast, lettuce, weak tea, white bread and butter.

2nd meal :—Welsh rarebit, tea, white bread and butter.

3rd meal :—Potatoes, cheese, white bread and butter, greens, rice pudding, stewed fruit.

Walked 17½ miles before first meal.

It will be noticed that I ate white bread. This was not because I prefer it, but I was obliged to eat it as none other could be obtained as a rule.

I eat always wholemeal bread at home.

The tea also was very weak indeed. Cocoa I found made me feel rather dull, when I had to walk after it. All the same I do not infer that tea is a good drink, but it was the best I could get on the way.

Sleep.

On an average, the whole walk through, I had less than seven hours sleep each night, and the last week less than six.

This was because the amount of time needed for walking, meals, baths, etc., left no longer than this for sleep. Otherwise I should have tried to have had eight hours each night.

Clothing.

My clothing consisted of a pair of light knickers, buckled below the knees, merina stockings, boots, specially made ; a light athletic jersey, with a collar buttoned to it ; check tie, a light alpaca jacket, with a sweater and pair of woollen gloves in readiness for cold weather.

❧ ❧

Baths.

Each night, with the exception of two, directly 1 had finished walking for the day a warm bath was taken. In this I lay for about two minutes and then washed all over with soap to take off the travel stains.

The days following the nights the bath was omitted I had terribly aching feet, caused by the presence of uric acid in the blood.

As I lay in the bath I could distinctly feel the uric acid leaving my body, and when I came out all heaviness had gone. This is something for people with rheumatic tendencies to reflect upon.

I was surprised myself at the difference the bath made. After the bath I rubbed my body all over with pure olive oil, nothing else.

Weight.

I lost little or no weight during the progress of the walk, although my face at the finish looked a little thinner. Four days after the finish I felt quite as fresh as at the commencement. For two or three days after the finish I ate and slept rather more than I usually do, but after that I was in a normal state in every way.

✶ ✶

List of Signatures.

1st day, Monday, Aug. 29th.

Land's End, 5 a.m.—

 Edwin Thomas, Land's End Temperance Hotel.

 Thos. W. Allen, 110 Upper Conduit St., Leicester.

Penzance, 7.20 a.m.—Mr. P. T. Laiton, A. Symes.

Hayle, 9 a.m.—Mr. E. Wollen, Mr. W. E. Burgess.

Cambourne, 10.45 a.m.—Mr. Sarkey.

Truro, 1.45 p.m.—Mr. T. Harriss.

Grampound, 4.50 p.m.—R. James.

St. Austell, 6.15 p.m.—Mr. C. Rowse.

(My attendant had omitted to take full signature (name and address) on the first day, but this was done from this point.)

2nd day, Tuesday, Aug. 30th.

St. Austell, 4.45 a.m.—

    Mr. B. Rabey, Market Hill, St. Austell.

    S. J. Menneai, Market Hill, St. Austell,

East Taphouse, 8.45 a.m.—

    Frederick Salt, baker, East Taphouse.

Liskeard, 11 a.m.—

    J. Richard, Four Mills.

Polhartic, 1.5 p.m.

    Mr. R. J. Parker, butcher, St. Germans.

Tor Point, 4.40 p.m.—

    W. Warrington, Tor Point.

Plymouth, 5.45 p.m.—

    N. S. Quartich, Plymouth.

3rd day, Wednesday, Aug. 31st.

Plymouth, 4.50 a.m.—

    Charles Copp, Westminster Hotel.

Totnes, 10.15 a.m.—

    Mr. B. Higham, 83 High Street.

Newton Abbott, 1.10 p.m.—

    E. Watts, 83 Walborough St.

Chudleigh, 2.40 p.m.—

    H. Heyward, Clifford Hotel.

Exeter, 6.15 p.m.—

    W. J. Gray, Osborne Hotel.

4th day, Thursday, September 1st.

Exeter, 4.45 a.m.—
    W. H. Sargent, Osborne Hotel.

Cullompton, 7.55 a.m.—
    Florence Maud Park, Fore St.

Wellington, 11.50 a.m.—
    C. E. Hall, 47 Mantle St.
    T. Evans, 13 George St.

Taunton, 1.35 p.m.—
    C. B. Bax, 62 Fore St.

Bridgwater, 5.45 p.m.—
    Harry Curry, Albany Hotel.

5th day, Friday, Sept. 2nd.

Bridgwater, 4.15 a.m.—
    Harry Curry, Albany Hotel.

Cross, 8.20 a.m.—
    Miss N. Howell, Moorland Restaurant.

Bristol, 1.20 p.m.—
    Mr. Carynge, 68 Redcliffe St.
    Herbert Francis Potter, 45 Beaconsfield
        Road, Knowle, near Bristol.

Stone, 7.35 p.m.—
    F. C. Anideves, Northland.
    W. H. Tayler, New Inn.

6th day, Saturday, Sept. 3rd.

Stone, 4.30 a.m.—W. H. Tayler, New Inn.

Gloucester, 8.35 a.m.—
    Miss Dunn, Northgate Restaurant.

Worcester, 4.15 p.m—
    H. Drain, Central Restaurant.

7th day, Monday, Sept. 5th.

Worcester, 4.20 a.m.—
    H. Drain, Central Restaurant.

Bromsgrove, 7.20 a.m.—
    H. Cartland, Police Station.

Northfield, 9 a.m.—
    F. Ketley, Northfield Institute.

Birmingham, 11 a.m.—
    H. Pratt, 100 Munster Road.

Aston, 11.20 a.m.—
    J. S. Michiel, Barton Arms.

Perry Bar, 11.35 a.m.
    W. Barnett, New Crown Inn.

Great Bar, 12.5 p.m.—
    S. Roberts, Scott Arms.

Walsall, 1 o'clock.—
    J. Bassit, Bushall St.

Cannock, 2.40 p.m.—
    M. Vaughan, Crown Hotel.

Penkridge, 5 p.m.—
    Michael Egan, Horse and Jockey.
Stafford, 6.5 p.m.
    George Butters, Eagle Hotel,

8th day, Tuesday, Sept. 6th.

Stafford, 4 a.m.—
    George Butters, Eagle Hotel.
Stone, 5.45 a.m.—
    George Garland, 90 Newcastle Road.
Newcastle-under-Lyne, 7.45 a.m.—
    George H. Poole, 80 Market Place.
Congleton, 11.35 a.m.—
    A. Duncan, Congleton.
Chelford, 12.30 p.m.—
    W. J. Goodwin Martin, Devonport Arms.
Alderley Edge, 3.20 p.m.—
    G. Dargans, London Road.
Wilmslow, 3.45 p.m.—
    J. Mottershead, The Grove.
Cheadle, 5.10 p.m.—
    Miss Hooley, Cities' Ltd. Restaurant.
Manchester (St. Ann's Square), 8.50 p.m.—
    W. Fulton, 43 Hampden St., Ardwick.
    Tom Jolley, 30 Tanners Lane, Pendleton.

9th day, Wednesday, Sept. 7th.

Seedley, 4 a.m.—
    Joe. Ackerley, 498 W. Liverpool Street.
Bolton. 6.30 a.m.—
    J. Smalley, 28 Victoria Grove.
Horwich, 7.50 a.m.—
    Alice Morris, S. & S. Café.
Arlington, 9.30 a.m.—
    Enoch Moss, Church Street.
Jarrow Bridge, 9.5 a.m.—
    John Warburton, Jarrow Bridge Hotel.
Chorley, 10 a.m.—
    Samuel Farnworth, 27 Leigh Row.
    James Galt, 126 Market Street.
Chorley, 10.20 a.m.—
    John Broughton, Parkers' Arms.
Whittle-le-Woods, 10.35 a.m.—
    W. Parkin, Show Hill.
Claxton Green, 11 a.m.—Stephen Turney.
Preston, 2.5 p.m.—
    Sybil Ingham, 150 Church Street.
    ,,   2.45 p.m.—J. Larthage, Grey Friars.
Myertcough, 3.30 p.m.—George Crane.
Garstang, 4.40 p.m.—
    Richard Salisbury. Bond Lane.
    ,,   4.45 p.m.—Arthur Gill, High Street.

Sabot, 5.25—J. G. Saul, Hamilton Arms Hotel
Golgate, 7.15 p.m.—
    William Hargraves, London Terrace.
Lancaster, 8.15 p.m.—
    B. Hamer, Elm House Hotel, Meeting
        House Lane.
    10th day, Thursday, Sept. 8th.
Lancaster, 5 a.m.—
    B. Hamer, Elm House Hotel.
Carnforth, 6.40 a.m.—
    James Jollys, 125 Hall Street.
Burton, 6.50 a.m.—
    Elizabeth Braithwaite, C. Bank.
Nr. Crooklands, 8.20 a.m.—
    William Phenson, postman.
Barrows Green, Nr. Kendal, 9.45 a.m.—
    Mary Anne Johnson, Punch Bowl Inn.
Kendal, 11.30 a.m.—
    Richard Pattison, 118 Kirkland Road,
        North Woodend, Railway Hotel,
Illside, 1.0 p.m.—
    George Mearns, ploughman.
Shap, 3.30 p.m.—
    Tom Conchie, Bull's Head.
Penrith, 7.15 p.m.—
    Miss Thistlethwaite, Exchange Hotel.

11th day, Friday, Sept. 9th.

Penrith, 3.55 a.m.—
  Miss Thistlethwaite, Exchange Hotel.
Low Hesket, 6.10 a.m.—T. Dunlop.
Wrigmire Moss, 7 a.m.—Jemima Potts.
Carlisle, 8.15 a.m.—T. Mills, Carlisle.
Gretna, 11.40 a.m.—
  Mrs. M'Cracken, Old Toll Bar.
Kirkpatrick, 12.40 p.m.—
  John Diris, Graham's Hill.
  William John Bell, Newton.
Ecclefechan, 2.30 p.m.—
  Kate Campbell, Bush Hotel.
St. Mungo, 4.10 p,m.—
  Kate M'Dougall, Castlemilk Smithie.
Lockerbie, 5.10 p.m.—
  Miss S. Carruthers, Muirhouse.
Johnstone Bridge, 6.35 p.m.—
  William Kinnsick, post office.
Beattock, 9.30 p.m.—
  Mrs. Charteris, Refreshment House.
  12th day, Saturday, Sept. 10th.
Beattock, 5.15 a.m,—Mrs. Charteris.
Darthope Viaduct, 7.10 a.m.—John Granger.
Elvanfoot, 8.27 a.m.—George Little.
Crawford, 9.4 a.m.—Hugh Stevenson.

Abington, 9.55 a.m.—
    Miss Polly Wellside, Abington Hotel.
12 o'clock.—James Lang, Newstables (no
    place given).
Douglas, 1.25 p.m.—
    James Crawford, Craig Burn.
Lesmahagow, 2.15 p.m.—James Summerville.
Larkhall, 4.30 p.m. — James Miller, Alex.
    Crichton, Agnes Miller, and 6 others.
Hamilton, 6.38 p.m.—Wm. Jones, Brandon.
Glasgow, 9.15 p.m.—J. J. M'Neil.
    John Elder, 43 Seamore Street.
13th day, Monday, Sept. 12th.
Glasgow, 5 a.m.—
    Mr. David J. Dor, 4 Milton St., Partick.
    Thos. Herbert, Marchill Riddrie.
Cumbernauld, 8.20 a.m.—
    L. J. Neilson, Lynn Hotel.
Dennyloanhead, 9.55 a.m.—James Dunnett.
Denny, 10.25 a.m.—W. Burty, 10 Stirling St.
St. Ninians, 11.40 a.m.—
    A. Macdonald, 16 Main St.
Stirling, 12.3 p.m.—
    William Kinnard, King's Stables.
Bridge-of-Allan, 12.50 p.m.—
    Mrs. A. S. Hunter, Zetland House.

Braco, 3.30 p.m.—
  Mrs. Lawrence, Balhaldie Toll.
Blackford, 4.55 p.m.—J. Gilmour, W. A. Gillis.
Auchterarder, 6 p.m.—
  Robert H. Clark, Coffee House.
Aberathven, 7.15 p.m.—
  Peter Stalker, sub-postmaster.
Perth, 9.45 p.m.—
  John Wilson, Waverley Hotel.
    14th day, Tuesday, Sept. 13th.
Perth. 5 a.m.—John Wilson, Waverley Hotel.
Stanley, 6.15 a.m.—Mrs. Louden, Mancehall.
Bankfoot.—Jimmie Stewart.
Dunkeld, 8.25 a.m.—
  Ian Dickson, Athol Arms Hotel.
Guay, 10.30 a.m.—James Douglas.
Ballinluig, 11.5 a.m.—J. J. Scott, The Store.
Pitlochry, 12.15 p.m.—
  Adam Doggart, Prospect House.
Blair Athole, 2.30 p.m.—
  George Elmslie, Tilt Hotel.
  R. Marshall, Bruai.
Calvine, 3.40 p.m.—
  J. Macpherson, Post Office.
Dalnacardock, 5.10 p.m.—Mary Watson.
Dalnaspidal, 6.30 p.m.—Mrs. Grant.

Dalwhinnie, 9.5 p.m.—
   Donald MacKenzie, Locheritch Hotel.
15th day, Wednesday, Sept. 14th.
Dalwhinnie, 5 a.m.—
   Donald MacKenzie, Locheritch Hotel.
Kingussie, 8.25 a.m.—
   John I. Macpherson, 39 Princes Street.
Kincraig, 10.50 a.m.—A.M. Cumming, Baldon.
Aviemore, 12 o'clock.—
   Rev. Alex. Rattray, Rignakyle.
   „   12.18 p.m.—M. Davidson.
Carrbridge, 1.40 p.m.—
   Lucy Grant, Carrbridge Hotel.
3.50 p.m.—Mary Anderson, (name of place
   indistinguishable).
——— Crossing, 4.10 p.m.—E. Macdonald.
Tomatin, 4.49 p.m.—James Cooper.
Coy, 5.50 p.m.—J. Hunter.
Craggie Inn, 7 p.m.—M. Fraser.
Inverness, 9.40 p.m.—
   Miss M'Gilvray,   Temperance   Hotel,
   Church Street.
   16th day, Thursday, Sept. 15th.
Inverness, 4.40 a.m.—No one up to sign.
   J. C. Elder went out three miles.
Inchmore, 6.45 a.m.—Donald M'Kenzie.

Muir of Ord. 8.30 a.m.—
    Annie Fraser, Station Hotel.
Conan Bridge, 10.25 a.m.—William M'Kenzie.
Dingwall, 11 a.m.—A. Nichol.
Waterton, 11.35 a.m.—Christina Macintosh.
Evanton (no time given).—Kenneth M'Kenzie.
Alness, 1.20 p.m.—
    Alex. M'Kay, The Manse.
Kilday, 3.40 p.m.—Ella M'Kenzie.
Tain, 5.55 p.m.—G. H. Shearer, sadler.
Mickle Ferry, 7.15 p.m.—
    R. M'Kenzie, ferryman.
Clashmore, 9 p.m.—Dolly M'Kay.
Golspie, 12.5 (midnight), Donald M'Kay.
    Mrs. Crane, Temperance Hotel.
      17th day, Friday, Sept. 16th.
Golspie, 6 a.m. (no one up to sign book).
Dunrobin, Golspie, 6.20 a.m.—Geo. Peterkin.
Brora, 7.35 a.m.—Wm. Grant, Rosslyn Street.
Crakaig Loth, 9.10 a.m.—R. W. M'Kay.
Helmsdale, 10.30 a.m.—
    Thomas M'Kay, Commercial Hotel.
Ansdale, 12.55 p.m.—A. Urquhart.
Berridale—Mrs. William Sutherland.
Dunbeath, 3.20 p.m.—
    (Name undiscipherable) Post Office.

Latheron Wheel Hotel, 3.5 p.m.—
  Cissie Sutherland.
Lybster, 6.15 p,m.—Alex. Quichan.
Mid Clyth, 7 p.m.—John Nicholson.
Wick, 9.35 p.m.—W. Randan, Station Hotel.
John o' Groat's, 2.33 a.m., September 17th.—
  Mrs. Calder, John o' Groat's House Hotel.

Some of the signatures were so indistinctly written that a few errors may have been made.

Appendix.

AT the conclusion of his walk Mr. George H. Allen was submitted to medical examination, and the following is the doctor's certificate :—

"GEORGE H. ALLEN, 37 years, 16th June, 1904, about 9 stone 4 lbs. 909½ miles, Land's End to John o' Groat's ; August 29th, 5 a.m. Did not walk any on the two intervening Sundays. Arrived at John o' Groat's at 2.33 a.m. Saturday, 17th September, doing journey in 16 days 21 hours 33 minutes, record by 7¼ days. Averaged 63 miles a day during the last five days and finished with 73½ miles on last day. Was training specially for 10 weeks prior, including his ordinary farm work. Has been an athlete for 21 years. Holds Leicester to London record, 97¾ miles, time 20 hours 22 minutes 25 seconds ; walked this without a stop. Also engaged in long-distance running, and won over 100 prizes in this but does not hold record. First began three years ago to walk very long distances, viz :—Leicester to Bedford and back—100 miles—22 hours 14 minutes : previous to that

50 most ever done. For past six years has been a Vegetarian. Chiefly garden vegetables and bread. Wheaten bread, home made. Very little fruit, as could not get it where he lives. Three meals a day during training, this his usual.

Breakfast—Ordinary—One or two cups very weak tea, about six slices bread and nut butter. Training—One or two boiled eggs additional (8 a.m.).

Dinner—(1 p.m.)—Garden vegetables with lentil rissoles *i.e.* with rice, cooked with little water. Bread—large bread eater. No fluids at dinner.

Tea—(6 p.m.)—Weak tea, bread and nut butter generally, and occasionally, but only occasionally, a little cheese. No milk partaken of.

During Walk—Every morning for

Breakfast—Poached eggs on toast, ordinary butter, white bread (only to be got) with weak tea

Dinner—Vegetables and stewed fruits and bread. No fluids.

Tea—Bread, butter, salad and weak tea.

Usually three meals on walk.

Never ate between meals while walking

Averaged over four miles an hour all the way

Rest—Never rested longer at a meal than 1

hours—average, under one hour. Never averaged more than five hours sleep, especially
during the last week. Slept sound and never
required to be wakened by any one. Accompanied during last week by two cyclists and an
advance agent, to arrange meals and accommodation.

Condition af Weather—

1st week	-	Too hot.
2nd week	-	Too wet.
3rd week	-	Perfect.

Roads—Good on the whole. Did not suffer
from the heat and never required to drink
between meals on route.

Personal History.— Occupation— Farming.
Up to 16 years of age in ill-health. Epileptic
(sister died of epilepsy)· He began about
eight years of age to have seizures. No other
ailments recollected ; becoming more frequent
till having 32 seizures in one day at age 16
years and not expected by doctor to recover.
Total abstainer and non-smoker all his life,
and at 16 went in for a rigid system of diet,
exercise and baths (cold), and after this had
only slight attacks, and never had an attack
since 18 years of age. Taken no medicine

since 16 years of age.   Does not now take
cold baths unless bathing mid-day occasionally
in the stream.   Warm baths taken two or three
times weekly.

General Appearance—Height, 5 ft. 4¾ in.;
sharp, intelligent young man ; brown hair, blue
eyes.   Always clothes very scantily, especially
when   at   home,   and   lives   practically in
the open air—often sleeping out-of-doors.
Self-trained.   He is of slender build, but every
muscle is well developed—not an ounce of fat.

     Chest expansion   -   34 – 36½
     Arm   -   -   -   10½– 11½
     Thigh -   -   -   18½– 18½
     Calf, right, *(digging)* 14″ – left, 13″.

No physical culture apparatus except natural
labour of the soil   No dumb-bells, etc.; grinds
wheat on mill and digging.   Each day after
bath rubs body with olive oil.   Heart and
lungs sound.   Back bronzed with sun from
labour.   He considers the mental strain more
than the physical.   Shoemaker by trade.
Followed trade up to 2½ years ago, and since
then took up the farming.   16–34 shoemaker
Exercise chiefly running, and marks the cure
of his ailment from these causes with aid of

mental efforts.   Feet in good condition.
Blistering very slight and last occurred during
last day of effort.   No *medicaments* used during walk and while training washing only in
warm water every night.   Bathed warm water
every night except two and felt effects of want
as on day following these two he felt his feet
aching. Boots 2 lbs. 4 ozs. Considering the
physique of the man it is marvellous that he
should be able to undertake the task which he
has just accomplished.   His physique follows
the feminine type which is borne out by the
above measurements.   His muscular system
is well developed, especially the muscle of the
thigh and calf of the leg.   The chest is well
developed.   The arms are not such as to call
for any particular remark.   As far as can be
judged from external appearance and a careful
examination there is no evidence of any ner-
vous lesion.   His boots had broad soles laced
down to near the toe, having rubber heels ;
knickers and cotton shirt ; Cashmere jacket."

(Signed)   JOHN McKIE, M.B., C.M.

26 Hillside Terrace, Springburn,
Glasgow, 19th September, 1904.

CPSIA information can be obtained
at www.ICGtesting.com
Printed in the USA
BVOW01s1508161116
468036BV00015B/194/P